ARE WE NEARLY THERE YET?

Brian Moses lives in Sussex with his wife and has two daughters. He travels the country performing his poems in schools and libraries. He once saw a driver of a car pull over on to the hard shoulder, get out of the car and do a war dance, probably in response to the two children in the back calling 'Are We Nearly There Yet?' for the twenty-seven millionth time!

Gunvor Edwards lives on a farm in the middle of a field. Her nearest neighbours are rabbits. She draws most days until teatime. After that she tends the ants, spiders, bats, woodworms, mice, nettles, cat and husband called Peter, who share the farm with her. Gunvor has illustrated many books for children, including another poetry anthology.

ARE WE NEARLY THERE YET?

Holiday Poems chosen by
BRIAN MOSES

Illustrated by Gunvor Edwards

MACMILLAN CHILDREN'S BOOKS

First published 2002 by Macmillan Children's Books

This edition published 2011 by Macmillan Children's Books
a division of Macmillan Publishers Limited
20 New Wharf Road, London N1 9RR
Basingstoke and Oxford
Associated companies throughout the world
www.panmacmillan.com

ISBN 978-1-4472-0170-0 (TRADE)
ISBN 978-1-4472-0015-4 (SPL)

3 5 7 9 8 6 4 2

A CIP catalogue record for this book is available from the British Library.

Printed and bound by CPI Group (UK) Ltd, Croydon, CR0 4YY

Contents

The Concise Guide for Travellers – *Roger McGough*   1

Impossible Journeys – *John Rice*   2

The Fabulous Four – *Marian Swinger*   4

Wizard's Holiday – *Roger Stevens*   6

Travelling – *Marian Swinger*   8

Common Sense? – *Clive Webster*   10

Holiday Booking Form – *Trevor Harvey*   12

Words to Pack a Suitcase – *Margaret Blount*   14

What We'd Really Like to do on

       Holiday . . . A Family Poem – *Paul Cookson*   15

Iceland – *Clare Bevan*   18

Recipe for a Rude Awakening – *Sue Cowling*   20

Setting Off – *John Coldwell*   22

The Travellin' Britain Rap – *Wes Magee*   23

Yellow Car, Yellow Car – *Sue Dymoke*   25

Going on Holiday – *Matt Simpson*   27

The Carousel – *Peter Dixon*   28

Coast Train – *Sue Dymoke*   29

Ferry Story – *Eric Finney*   30

Haute Cuisine – *Paul Bright*   32

London, Here I Come . . . – *Trevor Harvey*   34

The Haunted Hotel – *Marian Swinger*   35

I Love Our Orange Tent – *Berlie Doherty*   36

How to Open a Tin of Beans . . . – *Danielle Sensier*   38

Come Camping – *Daphne Kitching*   39

Postcard Home – *Kate Williams*   40

Things We Did in Scotland – *Brian Moses*   42

Driving Over the Mountains – *Kate Williams*   44

Duffle Bag – *John Coldwell*   45

Riding the Chair Lift – *Jan Dean*   46

Seaside Sonata – *Mary Green*   48

Elephants on the Beach – *Clare Bevan*   49

A Wave Like a Whale – *Joan Poulson*   52

Seaside Song – *John Rice*   55

Holiday Time – *Daphne Kitching*   57

The Concise Guide for Travellers

1. For covering long distances
   travel is a must.
2. Destinations are ideal places
   to head for.
3. By the time you get there
   abroad will have moved on.
4. To avoid jet lag
   travel the day before.
5. If you cross the equator
   go back and apologize.
6. If you meet an explorer
   you are lost.

Roger McGough

Impossible Journeys

I'll never walk the length of an African plain,
nor cross the Alps in a super-fast train.

I'll never take a taxi to Timbuktu
nor sail in a yacht to Tokyo Zoo.

I'll never parachute to descend on Crawley
nor travel with precision in a supermarket trolley.

I'll never see the grass of Savannah lands
nor the shimmering haze of the Kalahari sands.

I'll never ride a Greyhound through New York State
nor find the long-lost key to the Golden Gate.

I'll never board a jet to visit Hong Kong
nor take a slow boat to China to play ping-pong.

I'll never make another journey, you can ask me why,
because I've been everywhere . . . except Paraguay!

John Rice

The Fabulous Four

'It's been the usual hols,'
said Kate, sounding peeved.
'We've foiled several kidnappers,
   caught a few thieves,
   trapped master criminals,
helped with the chores,
   exposed a big smuggling ring,
   and stopped a small war.
   It goes without saying
that our superior brains
   have ensured that we've out-thought
   the cops yet again.
   We've found hidden treasure,
   had midnight feasts,
picnicked on Bodmin
and waylaid its Beast,
solved a couple of mysteries
   (child's play to us)
   and stopped, by quick thinking,
   a runaway bus.'
'As usual,' said Charles.

'Same old thing,' groaned Rashid.
'It's our curse,' said Danielle,
'that we always succeed.'
Off, rather glum, went
the Fabulous Four,
feeling that hols
were a bit of a bore.

Marian Swinger

Wizard's Holiday

Wizards on holiday
Never do spells
But keep their wands locked away
However tempted
They might be
To brighten a dull, rainy day

Roger Stevens

Travelling

Mum just loves travelling,
so does my dad,
and they drag me along with them,
travelling mad.
I've trekked through the rainforest,
covered in leeches
and blistered on boiling hot
tropical beaches.
I've been frozen in Greenland
and tossed upon waves,
trapped on the Eiger
and only just saved.
I've backpacked through Queensland.
It was there that I blubbed
when we were lost in the outback
and had to eat grubs.

Then in far-off Tibet
while riding a yak,
I broke both my legs
when I fell from its back,
but apart from the pain
it was all for the best
as now I'm in hospital
having a rest!

Marian Swinger

Common Sense?

Choosing a holiday,
Whad'ya know,
The usual question –
'Where shall we go?'

Will it be Spain
With a half-built hotel,
Or Florida sunshine,
Mosquitoes as well?

Will it be Portugal,
Potholes and all,
Or Texas with tower blocks
Twenty miles tall?

A trip on a river –
The Nile or Zambesi,
With head, legs and belly
Decidedly queasy?

Will it be Paris
Awash with its cars,
Will it be Mercury,
Venus or Mars?

Or will common sense
Tell us, 'No, let us spend
It somewhere between
John o'Groats and Lands End?'

Clive Webster

Holiday Booking Form

Help to find the hotel of your dreams by completing
the following form.

HOTEL REQUIREMENTS:

Hotel name	Hotel location	Date of arrival	How long (duration)
Bed and breakfast	Evening dinners	'Gourmet' banquets	Snacks (for slimmers?)
Special occasion	A business stay	Your annual break	A weekend away

ROOM SPECIFICATIONS:

Single only	Twin or double	Four-Star 'splendour'	Pile of rubble
Glimpse of mountain	Beach and yachts	View of car park	Chimney pots

FINALLY . . . INFORMATION ABOUT YOURSELF:

Loud and brash	Polite and sweet	May snore at night	Have smelly feet

THANK YOU *Have A Nice Stay!*

Trevor Harvey

12

Words to Pack a Suitcase

Press

Fold

Smooth

Roll

Tuck

Squeeze

Squash

Ram

Jam

Fit it in

Flatten

Now fasten.

Whew!

Margaret Blount

14

What We'd Really Like to do on Holiday ... A Family Poem

Swim and surf and splash and swim and slide and
    splash and swim
Wander round a stately home for an hour or two
Rollercoasters, helter skelters, big dippers, speedway
Walk up a hill and admire the lovely view

Bumper cars, waltzers, big wheels, ghost trains
Find an old museum and artistic gallery
Go-karts, trampolines, crazy golf, climbing frames
Sit down for a while with a nice cream tea

Arcades, slot machines, loud music, flashing lights
Look in all the quaint shops at paintings and antiques
Log flumes, motorboats, water-skis and water fights
Relax with a book on a nice deserted beach

Candy floss and ice creams, lollies, rock and sticky sweets
A five-course meal for two that takes at least three hours
Hot dogs, fish and chips, doughnuts, burgers
Ornamental gardens sniffing all the flowers

Pony rides, donkey rides, quad bikes, mountain bikes
Inspect the architecture in the older part of town
Roller-skating, roller-blading, ice skates and skateboards
Walk around cathedrals, not making a sound

Raves and discos, dancing and laser quest
Have a little picnic where no one is around
Cinemas and videos, karaoke talent shows
Spend hours at a medieval burial ground

Come on, Mum! Come on, Dad! There's loads and
    loads to do!
What we need's a holiday, a holiday from you!
Mum! Dad! Let's chill out and go somewhere
    dead cool . . .
You can go to Iceland and we'll stay by the pool.

Paul Cookson

Iceland

Iceland is the place to go
For sculptures carved from shining snow
Skilfully.

Iceland is the place for fools
Who splash around in outdoor pools
Wilfully.

Iceland is the place to be
For icebergs floating in the sea
Thrillingly.

Iceland is the place to choose
For glaciers and leaking shoes
Chillingly.

Iceland is the place to try
For nature's fireworks in the sky
Eerily.

Iceland is the place to find
White that burns your eyes, your mind
Blearily.

Iceland is the place for those
Who like to freeze their dripping nose
Rosily.

Iceland is the place for me
If I can watch it on TV
Cosily.

Clare Bevan

Recipe for a Rude Awakening

4 alarm clocks set for 2 a.m.
1 sister with wet sponge
no milk
1 pair of jeans (still in wash)
4 lost tickets
1 heavy downpour
1 late taxi

For the perfect start to your holiday mix the
first two ingredients with the rest of the family.

Find the no milk and the jeans.

Track down the lost tickets
while phoning the taxi company.

Wait till the downpour ends if possible. If not,
put on a brave face, cross fingers and . . . enjoy!

Sue Cowling

Setting Off

Holidays begin with
Tea, toast
And darkness.
Mum whispers,
'Quietly now, or you'll wake the neighbours.'
Like escaping prisoners we tiptoe towards the car
Where pillows and blankets wait silently on the back seats.

The car engine explodes into life
And we slide out into a night that belongs
To cats
And milkmen,
Where the road's black tongue
Slips beneath our wheels
And licks its lips.

John Coldwell

The Travellin' Britain Rap

All the drivers rattlin' on
in a million fast cars
drivin' up and down the country
like motor racin' stars,
on clearway,
    motorway,
        carriageway
           and street

then roundabout and road
through rain and hail and sleet,
drivin' up and down the country
till they're feelin' dead beat,
and the
    traffic noise,
        traffic noise
           has turned them half-deaf
so they take a Welcome Break
at Happy Eater, Little Chef

    and

        then

        they're

drivin' on, drivin' on
as the tyres zip and zap
through a thousand towns and cities
that are dotted on the map,
at least a million cars
– British, German, French and Jap,
    never stoppin'
          country hoppin'
              never stoppin'
                    country hoppin'
for all the cars are movin'
to the travellin' Britain rap,
for all the cars are movin'
to the travellin' Britain rap,
for all the cars are movin'
to

      the

   travellin'

      Britain

      rap.

          YEAH!

   *Wes Magee*

Yellow Car, Yellow Car

(For Declan and Conor)

Not metallic gold
    or bright lime green

Not screaming neon
    or deep, deep cream

Not sandy or bronze
    or even ecru

Not honey or mustard
    or ivory too

But yellow.

Not an ambulance
    or an AA van

Not a digger
    or a caravan

Not a lorry
    or a pick-up truck

Not a milk float –
    you're out of luck!

But a car
a yellow car
    yellow car

Found one?
    Seen one!

Winner!

Sue Dymoke

Going on Holiday

The engines are roaring,
The plane is soaring,
We're almost halfway to Spain!

Come on, jet!
I want to forget
The bad old English rain.

It's going to be fun
On the beach in the sun
With the sky as blue as can be.

I can't wait to land,
Get out on the sand
And splash like mad in the sea.

Matt Simpson

The Carousel

We're standing by the carousel
we're waiting for our case
my father's getting grumpy
– there's a scowl upon his face.

Our case is brown and oldie,
Dad's case is really bad,
he had it as a schoolboy,
he got it from his dad!

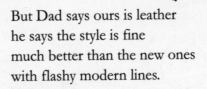

I wish we'd buy a proper case
like other families do,
slinky grey or scarlet,
orange, pink or blue.

But Dad says ours is leather
he says the style is fine
much better than the new ones
with flashy modern lines.

My sister thinks it's stolen
and so do Mum and Dad
but luggage thieves aren't crazy
and luggage thieves aren't mad.

Peter Dixon

Coast Train

Pigeons fly east with us:
an ever-flexing boomerang
across the fading blue.

Sometimes they race ahead
or swerve out of sight,
eyes on the warm loft at journey's end.

Across the aisle a woman writes letters home.
Her words are inky insects
scurrying across the ivory paper.

Opposite, an old man sleeps,
arms gripped round his chest,
dreaming of daughters far away.

A baby's cry is lost over the empty fields
and everything seems to turn back
except us,

our heads buzzing with excitement,
as we speed towards the start of
summer
and the afternoon sea.

Sue Dymoke

Ferry Story

The ferry doors open
Like a monster's jaw;
Car and lorry engines
Begin to rev and roar.
Out we all go from
Our floating park –
Just like the animals
Leaving Noah's Ark.
Out we go with never
A backward glance:
'We've made it,' says Dad,
'We're in France.'

Eric Finney

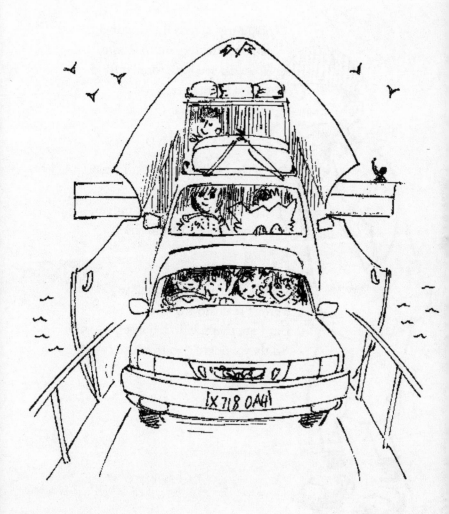

Haute Cuisine

Took a trip across the Channel,
From Amsterdam to Rome,
To see how foreign food
compares
With what I get at home.

In Holland they eat herring,
In a hundred different ways,
So I bought myself a burger,
The best I'd had for days.

Belgian fries with mayonnaise
Weren't really to my taste,
But I ate them, with a burger,
So they wouldn't go to waste.

French food, I'd heard, is 'magnifique!'
I really couldn't wait.
But I bought myself a burger,
And it wasn't all that great.

A real Italian pizza
Sounded just the thing, to me.
But the sign outside the burger bar
said 'Buy one – get one free!'

Took a trip across the Channel,
From Amsterdam to Rome,
But nothing beat the burgers
Mum cooked when I got home.

Paul Bright

London, Here I Come
(To See — and Not to Sea)

I'm on my way to LONDON . . .
It's meant to be a 'change'
From the Pleasure Beach at Blackpool
Or the golden sands at Grange;
The donkey rides at Weymouth
And the promenade at Rhyl,
Or the jellied eels at Yarmouth
(Of which I've had my fill!);
The sticks of rock at Brighton;
The amusements at Skegness;
The coloured sands at Alum Bay;
St Ives – and all the rest.

    'A week away in London,'
    My mum and dad agree,
    'Is something that we'll ALL enjoy' –

But nobody asked ME . . . !

Trevor Harvey

The Haunted Hotel

We stood, with our cases, ringing the bell
at the huge, studded door of our seaside hotel.
The door gave a creak, then it swung open wide.
A cadaverous crone cackled, 'Come on inside
and don't spoil the cobwebs, they go rather well
with the décor of our haunted hotel.'
As we crept up the stairs, we heard wailing and moaning
and a grey, wispy figure passed, rattling and groaning.
My brother screamed, 'Save me!' My sister went pale
as another faint figure proceeded to wail.
'Don't shun the ghosts, dear,' the ancient crone said,
'their feelings get hurt. They can't help being dead.
They've all been guests here at some time or other
and apart from the wailing, they're not any bother.'
Dad led the stampede as we raced for the door,
feet thudding frantically over the floor.
　　Panting, we hurtled away in the car.
　　　　'That,' said our mum, 'was never five-star.'
　　　　　'I agree,' said a voice from the boot,
　　　　　　where a ghost
　　　　　　　was perched on the luggage,
　　　　　　　'two-star at most!'

Marian Swinger

I Love Our Orange Tent

I love our orange tent.
We plant it like a flower in the field.
The grass smells sweet inside it.

And at night
When we're lying in it
I hear the owl crying.

When the wind blows
My tent flaps
Like a huge bird,
Like an orange owl.

And sometimes
I hear the rain
Pattering
Like little dancing feet.
And I feel warm and safe
Inside my tent.

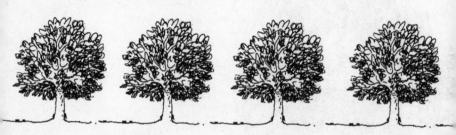

But when the sun shines – !
When I wake up
And the sun is shining
It pours like yellow honey over us.

I love my orange tent.

Berlie Doherty

How to Open a Tin of Beans on a Camping Trip with Your Brother (Who's Forgotten the Tin Opener)

Don't puncture it with tent pegs
Don't chuck it at a tree
Don't stamp on it with studded boots
Don't use your brother's teeth
Don't bash it with an angry stone
Don't try to talk it round

Stuff yourself with sweets instead and
open it back home.

Danielle Sensier

Come Camping

Come camping, come camping,
It's really great,
With spider-flavoured sausages
And slugs stuck to your plate.
There are earwigs in your Wellingtons
And ants sharing your bed,
The wasps you sprayed are fighting back
And targeting your head.
The hollow where you pitched your tent
Has turned into a bog,
And that dripping muddy monster
Is what used to be your dog.
Your clothes are cold and smelly,
Your sleeping bag feels damp,
It's a riot, it's sensational,
So come with us and camp!

Daphne Kitching

Postcard Home

Having a real break(down)
here! Spending all my ~~time~~ [money] in
this pretty ∧[awful] village.
Hotel staff great ∧[idiots]. Meals
terrific (disasters).
Weather ~~mild~~ [wild] and mountain
roads ~~charming~~ [alarming], so have had
some tremendous ~~drives over~~ [dives off]
the peaks.

...side's teeming
...h all kinds of
filth   smells
...sh and ~~shells~~.
　　Stressed
~~Stretched~~ out there today

　　Feeling set up already, and
　　　I wasn't
wishing ~~you were~~ here.

　　　　　Moaner
　　　　　~~Mona~~

Kate Williams

41

Things We Did in Scotland

Had high tea in Dalwhinnie,
rowed a boat upon Loch Linnie.

Watched the fishermen in Buckie,
went skiing near Glenduckie.

Bought a tiny tartan hankie
in a shop in Killiecrankie.

Took a walk near Inverdruie,
heard the pipes and drums in Muie.

Ate haggis in Dalmally,
saw eagles near Dowally.

Watched Highland Games in Braemar,
took presents home from Stranraer.

Thought we were in heaven
when we got to Kinlochleven,

and in Auchtermuchty town
we watched the sun go down.

But we didn't see the monster
in Loch Ness,

no, we didn't see the monster
in Loch Ness.

Brian Moses

Driving Over the Mountains

'Look at that beautiful,
heartlifting,
mind-blowing
view!'
called Dad from the front.

But all I could see
was the back of his head –
that shiny bald patch
to be blunt.

Kate Williams

Duffle Bag

If this poem was a duffle bag
I'd stuff it with sandwiches,
orange squash and a bar of mint cake
and I'd take it on a long, long walk.

After lunch I'd fill it with
the taste of clouds condensing on my face,
the rustle of small mammals in the bracken,
the surprise beyond the next hill.

And when I reached home
I'd sit in front of an open fire
and empty my bag very slowly.

John Coldwell

Riding the Chair Lift

Stand still
Here on this high hill
And wait
While the man hooks and turns
The swinging chair.
Stand still
Until it creeps right up behind you
The half-leap, half-hop
Hey-hup! Up!
Away into the air.

The ground not far beneath our swinging feet,
The sweet sound of birds and the quiet hum
Of the machinery that runs the lift . . .

Below, the earth shelves sharply
And suddenly we are sitting up in nowhere,
Our shoes above the trees,
Above the sparrows.
And we go slow. Oh, so slow.

Down over the wooded slopes
Where distant houses
Are like Lego bricks
Set in broccoli.
And the city is for dolls
And matchbox toys.
No bustle, no noise,
Only the great calm of the forest
And a steady floating joy.

Jan Dean

Seaside Sonata

To be sung on the way home

a caravan   a travelling man   a razor shell   kiss and tell

a ferry quay   a ruffled sea   knotted wrack   a chalk stack

fish bone   wish bone   high tide   slip'n'slide

kittiwake   waterscape   shore line   strandline

a brittle star   a limpet jar   a muffled bell   a sudden swell

a falling sea   anemone   a melody   a memory

Mary Green

Elephants on the Beach

It was just an ordinary
Not-too-chilly, not-too-breezy,
Not-too-sunny, not-too-hazy,
Not-too-anything
Seaside day.
The water splashed in the ordinary
Wavy way,
The sand stuck to our ordinary
Shivering skin,
The seagulls hung in the ordinary
Cloudy sky.

Then, as sudden as a rainstorm
And just as grey,
There were elephants on the beach.
Three astonishingly alien shapes
In wrinkled swimsuits
Slapped past the astonished crowds
To paddle in the surprised sea.
Three tails drew happy patterns
On the salty air,
Three trunks swung downwards
To hoover the ripples,
Three trunks snaked upwards
To shower the gulls with rainbows,
While we stared in fishy silence.

At last the world remembered to turn,
We remembered to breathe.
'There are elephants on the beach!'
Everyone shouted.
'Elephants!
On the beach!'
And we all stampeded,
Laughing for joy,
To follow the great, grey miracles
With their happy tails
And their trunks full of rainbows
Up the cliff path to the circus.

The tide did its best to wash their
    tracks away,
But the elephants have left
Extraordinary rock pools
That still shimmer in the sandy corners
Of our minds.

Clare Bevan

A Wave Like a Whale

It starts with us playing on the edge.
The sea is savage
and Dad begins swimming.
Don't go out there! Mum looks scared.

He's got medals, don't forget, Kev says.
But this is no leisure centre
– the sea here is like the inside
of a washing machine.

The tide's going out! Mum shouts.
Dad doesn't hear.
Our Shamina starts to cry.
Soft-head! Mum tries to smile.

I climb the rocks,
see Dad swimming . . .
further, further . . .
Then he turns.

He's coming back! I'm yelling
when a wave like a whale
eats him.
I think I scream.

Suddenly
I see him
and he's swimming . . .
swimming . . .

He really tries
— arms powerful scythes,
but it's like some sea-monster
has him on a line

towing him,
quite slowly,
sideways and round the point.
Out of sight.

Dad! I'm screaming. *Dad!*
Then I'm crying too
and I'm running, stumbling,
racing for where he disappeared.

And stop . . . daren't go closer.
I just stand there
and I'm shivering,
turning to look for Mum.

When
in the corner of my eye
there's a movement.
I swing round, see a head . . .

Dad!
scrambling into sight,
chest and arms clawed raw,
blood like becks . . .

But he's grinning . . .
and I'm in his arms.
Dad! You're alive!
It's Shamina yelling.

Yes, I am, love, Dad whispers.
Then they all fling on him
– me in the middle, squashed flat
as a jellyfish on the beach.

Better get you to hospital!
Mum says at last.
We're all looking at the blood.
Oh, no, not for that! Mum says.

It's a surgeon
your father needs.
A surgeon . . .
and a brain transplant!

Joan Poulson

54

Seaside Song

It was a
sun-boiled, bright light, fried egg, hot skin, sun-tanned
ssssizzzzzzler of a day.

It was a
pop song, ding-dong, candy floss, dodgem car, arcade, no
shade
smashing seaside town.

We had
a well time, a swell time, a real pell-mell time,
a fine time, a rhyme time, a super double-dime time.

We
beach swam, ate ham, gobbled up a chicken leg,
climbed trees, chased bees,
got stuck in sand up to our knees,
played chase, flew in space,
beat a seagull in a skating race,
rowed boats, quenched throats,
spent a load of £5 notes,
sang songs, hummed tunes,
played hide-and-seek in sandy dunes.

Did all these things
too much by far
that we fell asleep going back in the car
from the seaside.

John Rice

Holiday Time

Holiday time is different
To any other time.
It's made up of hours and minutes
Like all time is,
But somehow they rearrange themselves.
Holiday time is like elastic.
At the beginning of the holiday
The hours and minutes stretch out
So long that you think the days
Will go on for ever.
So much time ahead of you,
So many things you can do,
And you don't need to rush because
Time is just waiting for you,
Stretching out waiting . . .
Deliciously,
At the *beginning* of the holiday.
But, then before you know it
It's Thursday afternoon
And you go home on Saturday.
And all Friday will be taken up

With packing and tidying and buying presents.
And you still haven't been on a boat,
Or made yourself sick on the Super Looper,
Or flown the cockatoo kite you bought on Monday,
Or had a Knickerbocker Glory.
(You've *never* had a Knickerbocker Glory.)
Time – the elastic version – has caught you by surprise
And snapped back to a very short length.
It's strange,
But holiday time is different.

Daphne Kitching